T0359364

Could You Be an Astronaut?

Jill McDougall

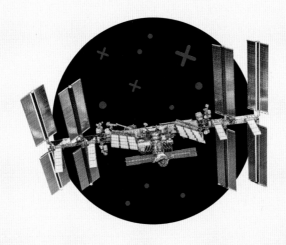

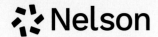

Could You Be an Astronaut?

Text: Jill McDougall
Publishers: Tania Mazzeo and Eliza Webb
Series consultant: Amanda Sutera
 Hands on Heads Consulting
Editor: Jarrah Moore
Project editor: Annabel Smith
Designer: Leigh Ashforth
Project designer: Danielle Maccarone
Illustrations: Fabian Slongo
Permissions researcher: Debbie Gallagher
Production controller: Renee Tome

Acknowledgements
We would like to thank the following for permission to reproduce
copyright material:

Front cover, p. 22: © Nexusplexus/Dreamstime.com; pp. 1, 24:
Shutterstock.com/Dima Zel; pp. 4, 5, 7 (inset), 8, 9 (top), 10, 11, 14, 17
(top), 19, 20, 21: NASA/JSC; p. 6: NASA/JSC/SpaceX; p. 7 (main): NASA/KSC;
p. 9 (bottom): NASA/JSC/Koichi Wakata; p. 13: NASA/MSFC; p. 15:
NASA/JSC/Mark T. Vande Hei; p. 17 (bottom): NASA/JSC/Scott Kelly; p. 23,
back cover: iStock.com/Naeblys.

Every effort has been made to trace and acknowledge copyright.
However, if any infringement has occurred, the publishers tender their
apologies and invite the copyright holders to contact them.

NovaStar

Text © 2024 Cengage Learning Australia Pty Limited
Illustrations © 2024 Cengage Learning Australia Pty Limited

Copyright Notice
This Work is copyright. No part of this Work may be reproduced, stored in a retrieval system,
or transmitted in any form or by any means without prior written permission of the
Publisher. Except as permitted under the *Copyright Act 1968*, for example any fair dealing for
the purposes of private study, research, criticism or review, subject to certain limitations.
These limitations include: Restricting the copying to a maximum of one chapter or 10% of this
book, whichever is greater; Providing an appropriate notice and warning with the copies of
the Work disseminated; Taking all reasonable steps to limit access to these copies to people
authorised to receive these copies; Ensuring you hold the appropriate Licences issued by the
Copyright Agency Limited ("CAL"), supply a remuneration notice to CAL and pay any required
fees.

ISBN 978 0 17 033404 4

Cengage Learning Australia
Level 5, 80 Dorcas Street
Southbank VIC 3006 Australia
Phone: 1300 790 853
Email: aust.nelsonprimary@cengage.com

For learning solutions, visit **cengage.com.au**

Printed in China by 1010 Printing International Ltd
1 2 3 4 5 6 7 28 27 26 25 24

*Nelson acknowledges the Traditional Owners and Custodians
of the lands of all First Nations Peoples. We pay respect
to Elders past and present, and extend that respect to
all First Nations Peoples today.*

Contents

A Home in Space   **4**

Working on the International Space Station   **10**

Keeping Fit   **14**

What's on the Menu?   **16**

Time for Sleep   **18**

A Long Way from Home   **20**

Could You Live in Space?   **22**

Glossary   **24**

Index   **24**

A Home in Space

Some astronauts live for months in a **spacecraft** high above Earth. These are the people who work on the International Space Station (known as the ISS).

So, what is the ISS? Here's the quick answer:

→ It's a large spacecraft that **orbits** Earth.

→ It's a home in space for astronauts.

→ It's a place where astronauts carry out **experiments**.

Could *you* live like an astronaut on the ISS?
Let's find out ...

An astronaut reads a book inside the ISS, high above Earth.

The ISS orbits Earth once every 90 minutes.

Life on the ISS is very different from life on Earth. You might be wondering what jobs you would do on board and what food you would eat. You might also wonder where you would sleep.

Are you ready to be **launched** into space? Then strap yourself in for a thrilling ride to the ISS! Be warned: the trip from Earth to the space station can sometimes take as long as three days.

An *International Space Station*

The astronauts living on the ISS come from many different countries.

Astronauts travel to the ISS in a small spacecraft.

The spacecraft is launched from Earth on the top of a powerful rocket.

The small spacecraft separates from the rocket after the launch.

Once you arrive on board the ISS, the first thing you'll notice is that you're floating! Why? Well, here above Earth, **gravity** isn't strong enough to pull you downwards. Low gravity is also called "micro-gravity" (*micro* means "very small").

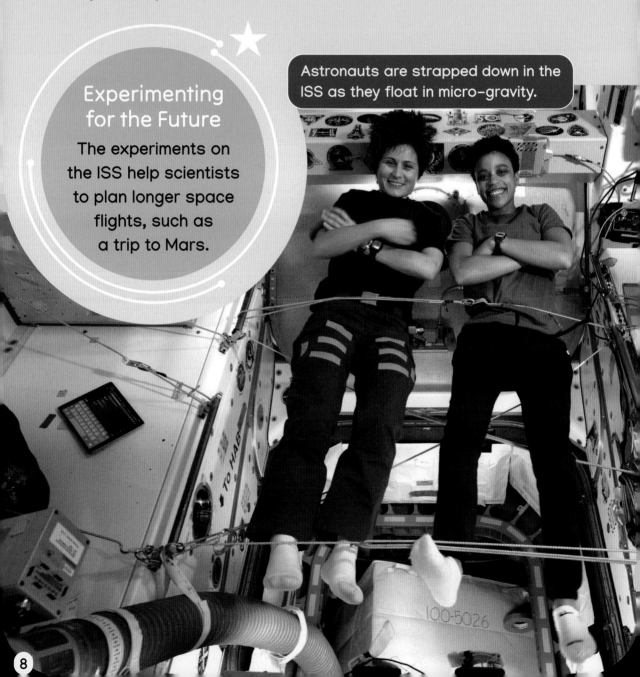

Experimenting for the Future

The experiments on the ISS help scientists to plan longer space flights, such as a trip to Mars.

Astronauts are strapped down in the ISS as they float in micro-gravity.

Astronauts experiment with growing plants without soil on the ISS.

The space station is the perfect place for scientists to find out how well people and other living things can survive in micro-gravity. So, while you're on the ISS, you'll take part in experiments to test things such as your fitness over time.

An astronaut takes part in a fitness experiment on the ISS.

Working on the International Space Station

You might think that you'd get bored living on the International Space Station, so far from Earth, but you'd be wrong! Astronauts on the ISS are very busy.

Here are a few jobs you might do:

→ Take a **spacewalk** to fix something on the outside of the space station.

→ Carry out science experiments.

→ Make a video for school children.

→ Clean the kitchen area (yes, really!).

An astronaut carries out an experiment into sound on the ISS.

An astronaut sets up an experiment into cooling on the ISS.

Hit the Books (and the Gym)!

Astronauts study and train for many years to work on the ISS.

Are you ready for your first job? Then put on your spacesuit, and let's go!

Here you are, standing outside the space station in your spacesuit. You're about to take a spacewalk to fix a part of the ISS that has stopped working properly. Your spacesuit has different parts to keep you safe.

Suit up!
The **life support system** in a spacesuit is worn like a backpack. It gives the suit power and gives the astronaut air to breathe.

PARTS OF A SPACESUIT

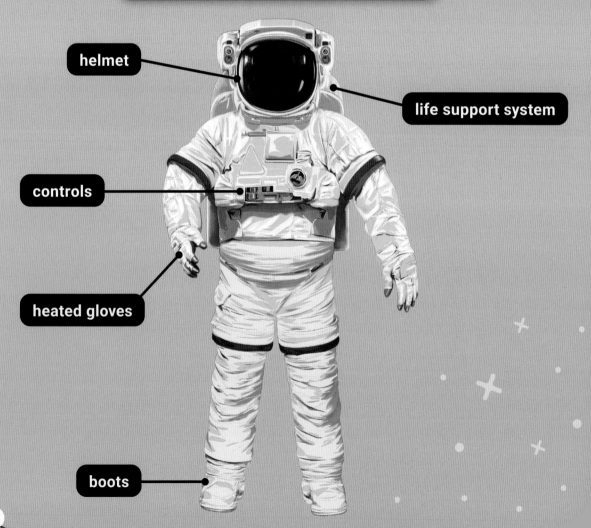

helmet

life support system

controls

heated gloves

boots

A spacewalk is not really a walk. It's more like a crawl.
Slowly, you creep towards the part that needs fixing.
All around you is the deep black of space – but don't panic.
You're tied to the spacecraft with a safety wire!

When you look down on Earth, you see mountains,
deserts and oceans. This is a moment you'll never forget!

An astronaut performs a
spacewalk outside the ISS.

Keeping **Fit**

It's important for astronauts on the International Space Station to keep fit. Since they move around by floating, their arms and legs become weak if they don't exercise every day.

In micro-gravity, astronauts can even float upside down!

There is a place on the ISS where astronauts can work out. Are you ready to get on the **treadmill** for a run? Make sure to strap yourself down first, or you'll float away.

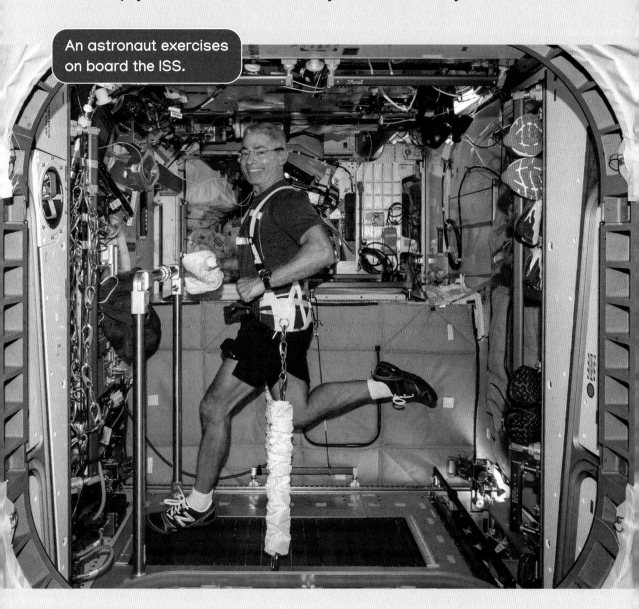

An astronaut exercises on board the ISS.

All that exercise will probably make you hungry, so keep reading to find out what you can eat on the ISS.

What's on the Menu?

Here's the good news: there are plenty of foods to choose from on the International Space Station menu. Many meals are cooked by chefs on Earth, then stored on the ISS in small pouches. Astronauts can heat up their food in a special food warmer.

TODAY'S MENU

Breakfast

scrambled eggs and apple juice

Lunch

vegetable soup

Dinner

rice and chicken

space station meals

Frozen Freshness

Many meals on the ISS are **freeze-dried** so they stay fresh and tasty.

But wait! Before you take a bite to eat, won't your food float away? Yes! You'll need to eat straight from the pouch, and use a special tube for drinks.

An astronaut drinks coffee from a pouch.

Time for Sleep

You might be surprised to discover that night and day come very quickly on the International Space Station. The ISS orbits Earth every 90 minutes. That means that when the space station is moving between Earth and the Sun, it is daytime on the ISS. Then, when the ISS moves into Earth's shadow, darkness falls.

Day and Night on the ISS

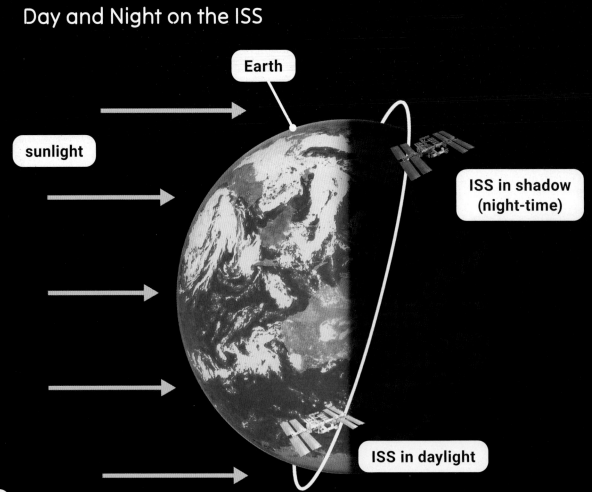

Earth

sunlight

ISS in shadow (night-time)

ISS in daylight

To get to sleep, you'll need a quiet space where you can shut out the light. Where will you go? Into your very own sleeping **pod**! Just clip your sleeping bag to a hook on the wall and ... float!

Sixteen Days in One

The astronauts on board the space station see 16 sunrises and sunsets every 24 hours.

An astronaut straps himself into a sleeping bag inside his sleeping pod.

A Long Way from Home

On the International Space Station, you'll be away from your family and friends for many months. Luckily, the computers on board have the internet, so you can chat with your loved ones.

Astronauts on the ISS chat with friends on Earth.

Astronauts on the ISS have fun together with a pizza party.

Astronauts on the ISS work together and they often have fun together, too. An astronaut named Scott Kelly once played a trick on the others by dressing up in a gorilla suit!

Mission Control, Do You Hear Me?

Astronauts on the ISS can speak to the **mission control centre** on Earth at any time. The control centre manages space flights from take-off until the end of each **mission**.

Could You Live in Space?

Life on the International Space Station could be a great adventure, but you might feel lonely at times, and even scared.

The men and women who live on the ISS can feel these things, too, but they have trained hard for life in space. These astronauts have a very important goal: to help us understand the mysteries of space.

Could you be one of them?

Glossary

experiments (*noun*)	tests done to try to learn something
freeze-dried (*verb*)	when food is frozen and then dried very quickly, to keep it fresh for a long time
gravity (*noun*)	the force that pulls objects towards Earth
launched (*verb*)	sent on your way to somewhere
life support system (*noun*)	equipment that keeps a person alive
mission (*noun*)	a trip into space
mission control centre (*noun*)	a place on Earth where people help the astronauts on a space mission
orbits (*verb*)	travels around a star, a planet or a moon
pod (*noun*)	a small part of a spacecraft that is separate from the main part
spacecraft (*noun*)	a vehicle used to travel in space
spacewalk (*noun*)	time spent outside a spacecraft, in space
treadmill (*noun*)	an exercise machine used for walking or running in one spot

Index

Earth   4, 5, 6, 7, 8, 10, 13, 16, 18, 20, 21, 24

exercise   14–15, 24

experiments   4, 8, 9, 10, 11, 24

family and friends   20

food   6, 16–17, 24

jobs   6, 10–11

micro-gravity   8, 9, 14

plants   9

sleep   6, 18–19

spacecraft   4, 6, 7, 13, 24

spacesuit   11, 12

spacewalk   10, 12–13, 24

Sun   18